NATIONAL
GEOGRAPHIC
KiDS

EVERYTHING
SHARKS

EVERYTHING SHARKS

BY RUTH A. MUSGRAVE

NATIONAL GEOGRAPHIC
WASHINGTON, D.C.

CONTENTS

This eye-catching shark is found around the world near tropical islands and is known by many names, including tiburón de Galápagos, manô, Galapagoshaai, and Galápagos shark.

A blacktip reef shark gliding along the coast of Tuamotu Archipelago, French Polynesia.

INTRODUCTION

STRUTTING THROUGH
THE OCEAN LIKE THE ULTIMATE ROCK STAR,
sharks are elegant, dynamic, sophisticated predators with a dangerous reputation. Sharks are completely unaware of how they inspire and intimidate. (Or maybe they're just too cool to care!)

What makes sharks so awe inspiring? From nose to tail a shark's entire body is engineered for survival.

Unfortunately, there's an ugly side to fame and it's taking its toll on these superstars of the sea. To appreciate and save them, you really need to know EVERYTHING about sharks.

EXPLORERS' CORNER

Hi! I'm Jennifer Hayes. And I'm David Doubilet.

Photographing and studying sharks has been our love and work for most of our lives. Sometimes it seems as if we're underwater more than above, but you'll understand why once you catch a glimpse of these magnificent animals. Look for this cartoon of David in the shark cage to indicate an Explorers' Corner where we'll share our experiences with sharks in the sea.

With teeth up to five centimetres tall, the white shark has the largest teeth of any living shark.

1

MEET
THE
SHARK

WHAT IS A SHARK?

FISH

SHARK

FISH

NOT A
SHARK

YOUR PET GOLDFISH MAY NOT
LOOK LIKE A (GREAT) WHITE, BUT IF YOU IGNORE THE
big teeth and bad reputation (and squint a bit. . .) you'll see the resemblance.
That's because sharks and goldfish are both fish.

Fish live in the water, have gills (to breathe), and fins. Most fish, including
sharks, have scales. There are about 32,000 kinds of fish found throughout
the world. Even on its most ferocious day, though, no one could confuse a
goldfish with a shark. A shark, and its close cousins rays and skates, are
fish, but a different kind. How are sharks different from a typical fish?

THRILL OF THE GILL

A shark has five to seven gill slits (openings) on each side of its head. A bony fish has just one.

NOTHING IS PERMANENT

A shark's scales and teeth are not permanent. It loses and regrows them throughout its life.

BONELESS FISH

Unlike most fish, a shark's skeleton is made of cartilage (like your ear or nose bridge), not bone.

FIRM FINS

The rigid fins and tail of a shark do not bend, flutter or fold up against the body like a bony fish.

BONELESS = AGELESS?

Scientists use bone, teeth or scales to determine the age of a bony fish. Without bones or permanent teeth and scales, it is a challenge to determine the age and life span of sharks.

5 REASONS IT'S GOOD TO BE A SHARK

1 You're more famous than a rock star.

2 Your reputation is fierce.

3 You never have to brush your teeth or visit a dentist.

4 You have the most awesome and awe-inspiring dorsal fins in the sea.

5 You like school but never have homework.

SHARK BITE
RED TAIL SHARKS, POPULAR IN HOME AQUARIUMS, ARE BONY FISH, NOT SHARKS.

SUPER SHARK AWARDS

FASTER THAN A SPEEDING

BULLETFISH, LEAPING SMALL BOATS IN A SINGLE
bound. . . it's super shark. Most of the 450 to 500 shark species go about their lives in secrecy, but a few stand out. Here are some of the world's super sharks.

BEST BURP (AND BARK)

When threatened, a swell shark doubles its size by gulping water. Once safe it makes a dog-like bark and burps out all the water.

SHARK REVO-LUTION

Whirling like a top, a spinner shark snaps up schooling fish with such power it vaults out of the water, making two to four full spins midair.

FAN-TASTIC FISH

Whale sharks are the world's largest shark—and fish. Possibly reaching lengths up to 20 metres (65 feet), it's larger than two buses. Weighing up to 34,006 kilograms (74,970 lbs), it doesn't just tip the scales, it smashes them!

SHARK BITE   IT WOULD TAKE 117 DWARF LANTERNSHARKS (OR PENCILS) TO BE AS LONG AS A WHALE SHARK!

SPEED CHASER

Shredding the water at 50 kilometres per hour (31 mph), a shortfin mako shark is the world's fastest shark. Makos are faster than bottlenose dolphins (35 kph/22 mph) and killer whales (48 kph/30 mph). Their speed makes them too fast for most predators—except humans.

During the day, as many as 36 nurse sharks pile on top of each other as they rest in caves and crevices.

BEST PILE

One of the smallest sharks, the dwarf lanternshark is only 17 to 20 centimetres (6.6 - 7.8 inches)—about as long as a pencil.

WEENY PREDATORS

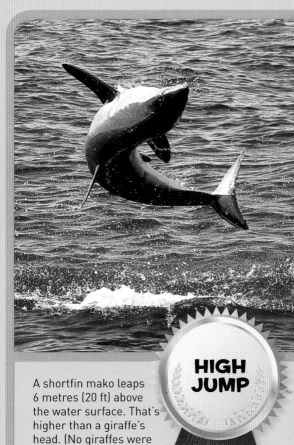

HIGH JUMP

A shortfin mako leaps 6 metres (20 ft) above the water surface. That's higher than a giraffe's head. (No giraffes were hurt making this comparison.)

EXPLORERS' CORNER

The most dramatic thing in the ocean is a shark. White sharks appear and disappear like ghosts. A shark cage is the only safe way to observe and photograph larger, more aggressive sharks. It's especially unwise to get out if there is more than one shark!

COOL SHARKS NEAR YOU

DIVE A METRE OR A MILE,
AND YOU WILL FIND A

.shark. Here are some exquisite examples of these elegant animals' ecosystems.

Usually found in water less than 4 metres (13 ft) deep, the **LEOPARD SHARK** is common along the Pacific coast of North America from Oregon to Mexico.

Little is known about the dazzling **ZEBRA BULLHEAD SHARK** found along the coasts of Japan, China, Taiwan, Vietnam and Australia.

The **TASSELLED WOBBEGONG** adds even more beauty to the coral reefs of New Guinea and Australia. It curls up in caves during the day and may eat any fish trying to share the space.

The **PRICKLY DOGFISH** gets its name from its super-rough scales. The best way to see this shark is from a deep-sea submersible off the coasts of New Zealand and Australia.

WORLDWIDE SHARKS

WHITE
Whether it's in the middle of the ocean or near the coast, white sharks (also called great whites) are found in nearly every ocean of the world.

LEMON
Lemon sharks hang out along the coast in waters as deep as 90 metres (295 ft).

SCALLOPED HAMMERHEAD
Scalloped hammerhead sharks live close to shore throughout the world.

TIGER SHARK
Tiger sharks are found throughout the world in temperate and tropical seas.

WHALE SHARK
The giant of the sea, the whale shark lives in tropical and temperate waters worldwide.

ARCTIC OCEAN

NORTH AMERICA

EUROPE

ATLANTIC OCEAN

AFRICA

SOUTH AMERICA

INDIAN OCEAN

ANTARCTICA

BASKING SHARKS are often seen off the coast of Britain. Over 20 species of shark live in British waters.

GREENLAND SHARKS chill in the North Atlantic and Arctic dining on seabirds, invertebrates and dead whales. Indigenous people have used its hide for boots and teeth as knives.

One place to see groups of **SPINNER SHARKS** hunting schools of fish is in warm-temperate and tropical waters of the Mediterranean.

The **NURSE SHARK** is active at night in the mangroves, reefs, and rocky shores of the eastern and western Atlantic, the Gulf of Mexico and the eastern Pacific from Mexico to Peru.

This stunning beauty is a **PYJAMA SHARK** found along the southern tip of Africa. Don't let its looks fool you. It eats hagfish, bony fish, small sharks and shark egg cases.

The **BLACKTIP REEF SHARK** is a common shark in the reefs of the Mediterranean Sea, and Pacific and Indian Oceans.

Map Key

- [ ] Polar waters
- [ ] Temperate waters
- [ ] Tropical and Subtropical waters

SHARK BITE SIX RARE SHARK SPECIES CALL THE FRESHWATER RIVERS OF BORNEO, AUSTRALIA AND INDIA HOME.

FROM SHORE TO OCEAN FLOOR

0 m (0 ft)

10 m (33 ft)

20 m (66 ft)

30 m (98 ft)

40 m (131 ft)

50 m (164 ft)

60 m (197 ft)

70 m (230 ft)

80 m (262 ft)

90 m (295 ft)

SHARK BITES
OFTEN HAPPEN WHEN PEOPLE ACCIDENTALLY TRIP OR STAMP ON A SHARK AT THE BEACH.

Baby Pool

Bays, inlets and shallow nearshore waters are important shark nurseries where pups can grow up away from larger predators. In one bay in the Gulf of Mexico, scientists found seven species of shark pups: blacktip reef, Atlantic sharpnose, bull, finetooth, bonnethead, scalloped hammerhead and spinner.

Bonnethead Shark

Beach Buddies

Paddlers, surfers and divers in Florida, U.S.A. are usually unaware that swimming nearby are sand devils, bonnethead, blacktip, sandbar, spinner, scalloped hammerhead and more.

Blacktip Reef Shark

Colourful Coral Sharks

Some might think sharks come in three colours: grey, light grey, and dark grey. But sharks that live in coral reefs dress for success with colour and pattern.

Puffadder Shyshark

SHARK BITE THE GREAT LANTERNSHARK LIVES 4,500 METRES (14,764 FT) DOWN—MORE THAN TWICE AS DEEP AS THE GRAND CANYON.

Wild Numbers

THERE'S ALWAYS

A SHARK NEARBY. Some sharks, like salmon, white and whale, migrate long distances through different habitats. Others stay close to home.

49 megamouth sharks have been documented since first discovered in 1976.

95 percent of the oceans have yet to be explored.

100 species of sharks are hunted for their fins, meat, oil and body parts.

3,800 metres (12,000 ft) is the average ocean depth.

11,100 kilometres (6,897 miles) in 99 days is how far and fast white sharks migrate from South Africa to Australia.

900,000 tons of sharks have officially been caught every year for the last 20 years. (Scientists suspect twice as many have actually been caught.)

Kelp forest

Sharks of the Forest

Around the British Isles coast, forests of giant seaweed called kelp provide a perfect home for thousands of Britain's sharks. Marine biologists claim the kelp is being wiped out by human activities.

Sharks in the Dark

Dive down 90 metres (295 ft) and the sunlight is 10 percent as bright as it was at the surface. At 150 metres (492 ft) you've lost 99 percent of the sunlight. Many sharks live even deeper where there is no sunlight at all. Even there, human activities such as fishing, pollution and oil spills threaten their survival.

Megamouth Shark

A PHOTOGRAPHIC DIAGRAM

SHARK PARTS

Scales The scales are like tiny teeth, with a pulp cavity and enamel layer.

Liver The fat-filled liver provides buoyancy and stores energy. A basking shark's liver is 25 percent of its body weight.

Camouflage Sharks virtually disappear above and below. The darker back blends in to the dark sea below. The light-coloured underside disappears in the lighter surface above. This camouflage is called countershading.

Skin Thick skin and scratchy scales make a shark's skin rough and tough. Some sharks, like carpet sharks, can change their skin colour to blend into their surroundings.

Fins Fins help with stability and manoeuverability, provide lift and propel the shark through the water. The size and shape depends on the shark's lifestyle.

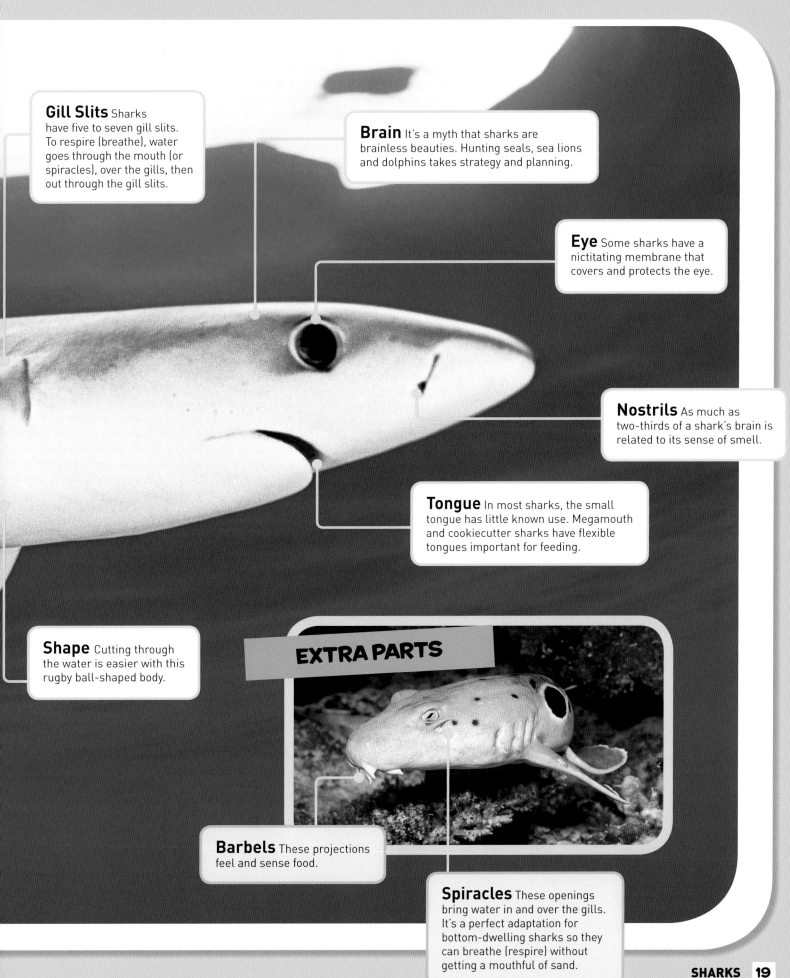

Gill Slits Sharks have five to seven gill slits. To respire (breathe), water goes through the mouth (or spiracles), over the gills, then out through the gill slits.

Brain It's a myth that sharks are brainless beauties. Hunting seals, sea lions and dolphins takes strategy and planning.

Eye Some sharks have a nictitating membrane that covers and protects the eye.

Nostrils As much as two-thirds of a shark's brain is related to its sense of smell.

Tongue In most sharks, the small tongue has little known use. Megamouth and cookiecutter sharks have flexible tongues important for feeding.

Shape Cutting through the water is easier with this rugby ball-shaped body.

EXTRA PARTS

Barbels These projections feel and sense food.

Spiracles These openings bring water in and over the gills. It's a perfect adaptation for bottom-dwelling sharks so they can breathe (respire) without getting a mouthful of sand.

2

IT'S A SHARK'S LIFE

Most sharks are finicky eaters. But the tiger shark gobbles up fish, other sharks, seabirds, iguanas, sea snakes, sea turtles and sea scraps such as rubbish and carrion.

OH, BABY!

IF SHARKS COULD TALK,

'MUMMY' AND 'DADDY' WOULD NOT BE IN THEIR vocabulary. Sharks do not care for pups or guard eggs. Unlike bony fish, sharks do not have a larval stage. All pups come into the world a fully formed predator with a mouth full of teeth ready to hunt. Exactly how they come into the world varies. Some are born live, others hatch from an egg, and some do both!

A peek inside a dogfish shark's egg case shows the yolk sac attached to the pup.

IT'S NEVER A GOOD IDEA TO TICKLE A BABY SHARK UNDER ITS CHIN. SCIENTISTS **HAVE BEEN BITTEN** BY UNBORN SANDTIGER SHARKS WHILE EXAMINING THE MOTHER.

SOME SHARKS HATCH FROM AN EGG . . .

Many sharks hatch from a leathery egg. The developing pup gets all its nutrients from the yolk sac. Depending on the species and water temperature, some pups hatch in a month; others take more than a year.
Examples: Horn, bull and swell sharks

Shark Pup

Yolk Sac

SHARK BITE WATER TEMPERATURE PLAYS AN IMPORTANT ROLE IN HOW QUICKLY THE EMBRYO HATCHES OR IS BORN.

YOU MUST BE YOLKING!

Sometimes one yolk isn't enough to grow on. In some species, when the embryo is the size of a paper clip, after it absorbs its own yolk, it eats the other eggs inside the female. Some species produce special eggs just for the embryos to eat. The sand tiger shark takes this up a notch. When the sand tiger embryo is about 10 centimetres (4 inches) long, it begins killing and eating the other embryos (inside the female). At birth, the surviving well-fed pup is 1 metre (3 ft) long and is almost half the mother's size.

. . .SOME SHARKS ARE BORN LIVE. . .

Similar to a mammal, the developing pups get their nutrients from the mother. This style of birth allows the mother to successfully give birth to large litters.
Examples: blue and hammerhead

Newborn Numbers

6 centimetres (2.4 inches) long is the size of newborn dwarf lanternsharks and thorny lanternsharks.

64 centimetres (25 inches) is the length of a newborn whale shark.

300 eggs were found inside one female whale shark.

135 blue sharks were born in one litter.

24 months is the longest (documented) shark pregnancy.

. . .AND SOME ARE BORN THROUGH A COMBINATION OF BOTH!

A third group have an interesting combo of egg and live birth. Rather than releasing the egg into the ocean, the fertilised egg stays inside the female. The embryo gets its nutrients from the yolk sac, hatches and is completely developed before it is born live.
Examples: whale sharks and spiny dogfish

A lemon shark and newborn lemon shark pup.

MAKING SENSE OF SHARK SENSES

IF THE CURRENT AND LIGHT ARE JUST RIGHT, A SHARK . . .

hears prey 250 metres (820 ft) away.

smells blood one kilometre (0.5 of a mile) away.

sees movement up to 15 metres (50 ft) away.

feels the flutter of moving animals one to two body lengths away.

detects living animals from 50 centimetres (20 inches) away.

ONE WAY TO GET A SHARK'S
ATTENTION IS TO SWIM LIKE A WOUNDED ANIMAL....

or a person. Sounds of thrashing made by an injured animal attract sharks. People flounder and wallow like wounded prey rather than slip through the water like a healthy seal or fish. Sharks take notice of more than just sounds. They're attracted to smell, movement and other signs of life. Check out sharks' mind-boggling senses.

LATERAL LINE A fluid filled canal, called the lateral line, runs down each side of a shark's body. The lateral line feels movement and vibration. The lateral line and sense of smell may work together to track ripples and scent made by moving fish.

SHARK BITE WHITE AND OCEANIC WHITETIP SHARKS POKE THEIR HEADS OUT OF THE WATER TO PICK UP AIRBORNE SCENTS.

AMPULLAE Freckling the shark's snout are *ampullae of Lorenzini*. These are small sensory pits that detect electrical currents radiating from all (living) animals. This sense locates prey buried in sand, for example.

EYES In the light, our vision is about the same as a shark's. In the dark, however, a shark's eyes are ten times more sensitive to light. Reflective cells (called tapetum lucidum) in the back of the eye work like a mirror to reflect and double the available light.

NOSTRILS A shark's sense of smell is 10,000 times better than ours! Sharks use ocean currents to pick up scents from further away. (Just as a breeze could lead you to a garden BBQ.)

TASTE Do sharks savour the fish flavour? Scientists are unsure. Some sharks may use taste to decide if something is edible. Some sharks may use taste and smell together to find food. Maybe you can figure out how to run a shark taste test!

EXPLORERS' CORNER

Because sharks see contrasting colours well, we never wear a shark's favourite colour, *yum yum yellow*. The lighter colour shows up too well against the darker ocean water. When wearing dark wetsuits, we cover up our hands and legs so they don't look like flashes of fish. Sometimes sharks bite our strobe lights because they're attracted to the electrical pulse. They lose interest after tasting the hard plastic.

OCEAN EATS

Though a few sharks hunt large prey such as seals or whales, most hunt and eat much smaller prey. Below is a partial list of what various sharks throughout the world might eat.

1. sharks, sharks, and more sharks (some listed below)
2. abalones
3. anchovies
4. angel sharks
5. barracuda
6. basking sharks
7. billfish
8. bonitos
9. bluefish
10. blue sharks
11. butterfish
12. caribou
13. catsharks
14. chimaeras
15. cod
16. corals
17. cownose rays
18. crabs
19. croakers
20. cuttlefish
21. dogfish sharks
22. dolphins
23. eagle rays
24. eels
25. elephant fish
26. elephant seals
27. flatfish
28. flounder
29. fur seals
30. giant squid
31. grey whale calves
32. grunters
33. guitarfish
34. hakes
35. halibut
36. hammerheads
37. harbour seals
38. hermit crabs
39. herring
40. horseshoe crabs
41. houndsharks
42. jellyfish
43. krill
44. lancetfish
45. lanternfish
46. lanternsharks
47. lizardfish
48. lobsters
49. lumpfish
50. mackerels
51. mako sharks
52. marlins
53. mullet
54. needlefish
55. penguins
56. ocean sunfish
57. octopuses
58. oysters
59. parrotfish
60. pollocks
61. porcupinefish
62. porpoises
63. prawns
64. pufferfish
65. rays
66. remoras
67. rockfish
68. rubbish
69. sailfish
70. salmon
71. sardines
72. scorpionfish
73. sculpins
74. sea anemone
75. seabirds
76. sea horses
77. sea lions
78. sea robins
79. sea snakes
80. sea squirts
81. sea turtles
82. sea urchins
83. seals
84. skates
85. skipjacks
86. smelts
87. snails
88. snappers
89. squid
90. squirrelfish
91. soldierfish
92. sole
93. steelhead trout
94. surgeonfish
95. swordfish
96. striped bass
97. tuna
98. whale calves
99. whiting
100. worms (polychaetes)
101. wrasses

People are not on any shark's menu! Bites are usually accidental. Find out more on pages 38–39.

EATING IN STYLE

SO MANY SHARKS,

SO MUCH STYLE. HOW A SHARK HUNTS AND WHAT IT EATS DEPENDS ON THE SHAPE AND SIZE of its body and teeth. Schools of sardines, mackerels, anchovies or herring become a swirling buffet for some sharks. Porbeagle, silky and other sharks rocket through fish schools gobbling up dinner. Makos and blacktip reef sharks do a little dinner prep by herding fish into a tight ball.

SCANNERS

Like a living metal detector, a hammerhead shark skims along the ocean bottom, using its ampullae of Lorenzini to scan for prey hidden under the sand.

SHARK BITE   A MAJOR PREDATOR OF MANY SHARKS IS ANOTHER SHARK.

STRAINING TO EAT

Whale, basking and megamouth sharks filter fish and plankton from the ocean.

HIDE AND EAT

Wobbegongs blend into the ocean bottom, watching and waiting for prey to swim close enough to snatch.

SNEAK ATTACK!

Looking upward in search of the perfect silhouette, some sharks, including the white and tiger, lurk just deep enough to hide in the dark. When a fish, seal or turtle swims overhead, the shark launches upward in a surprise attack.

OPEN WIDER?

As if a mouth full of razor-sharp teeth isn't enough, some sharks have a jaw-dropping ability. Really, their jaws drop! Unlike mammals, the shark's upper jaw is not fused to the skull. When biting, the upper and lower jaws drop and move forward, rotating the teeth outward. This gives the shark a larger bite or better suction to capture prey.

School Food

Sand tigers eat fish such as herring, snappers, remoras, eels and bonitos.

SHARK BITE   SCIENTISTS CAN IDENTIFY THE SPECIES BY THE TOOTH AND BITE SHAPE.

BITES WITH PEARLY WHITES

A SHARK WOULD BANKRUPT THE TOOTH FAIRY.

THROUGHOUT ITS LIFE, A SHARK MIGHT LOSE 30,000 TEETH!

Sharks have rows and rows of teeth and not one is permanent. Pups even lose teeth before they're born. When a tooth falls out, one from the row behind replaces it. Depending on the species, a tooth may last a week or a few months. Sharks do not chew their food; they swallow it whole or in chunks. According to the food it eats, a shark's teeth are designed to slice, rip, tear, or crush food.

Fast Food

Makos snatch fast-swimming swordfish and tuna with spearlike teeth.

Cracked Crab

Horn sharks have two kinds of teeth. The front teeth hold prey, the back grind. They eat crabs, prawns, sea urchins, sea stars, and small fish.

Supersize Meal

A white shark's teeth are serrated like a knife. It hunts large prey such as seals and sea lions.

Dine and Dash

The 48-centimetres-long (19 inch) cookiecutter hunts whales, tuna, marlin and basking sharks. This quirky predator doesn't eat the entire prey, just a bite. Using its lips for suction and teeth for drilling, it bores out a chunk of flesh, leaving behind a small hole as seen in this dolphin below.

Tooth Totals

30,000 teeth are lost throughout a shark's life.

3,000 tiny teeth inside a whale shark's mouth

8-10 days to grow a new tooth

3 millimetres (eighth of inch) is the size of a whale shark's tooth.

A PHOTO GALLERY

SHARKS ALIVE!

SHARKS.
SO MANY SHAPES AND SIZES.

Here's a shout out to some of the many incredible sharks from around the world.

Silky sharks and yellowtail snappers dining together in the waters off the coast of Cuba.

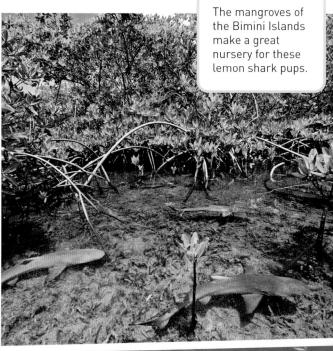

The mangroves of the Bimini Islands make a great nursery for these lemon shark pups.

This newborn Port Jackson shark pup is about 24 centimetres (9 inches) long.

Scientists captured this photo of a white shark breaching as it grabs a seal decoy in False Bay, South Africa.

Oceanic whitetip sharks are inquisitive, bold and sometimes aggressive if divers aren't careful.

A whale shark's mouth is 1.4 metre (4.6 ft) wide, almost as wide as a car.

This horn shark pup is in the middle of hatching from its spiral egg case.

The hammerhead shark's tough-as-nails reputation is false. They are wary and avoid people.

Luckily, this diver's close encounter with a white shark ended well. An adult white shark is more than three times longer than a person.

Adult sixgill sharks reach lengths up to 4.8 metres (15 ft) and hunt whales and seals. Smaller sixgills hunt rays, sharks and fish.

To find prey, a nurse shark uses its snout to root through the sand.

This swirling school of whitetip reef sharks searches for food.

SHARK SCHOOL

SHARK FAMILY TREE

Splitsville
More than 400 million years ago, fish-like creatures separated into two groups that still survive today: Osteichthyes (bony fish) and Chondrichthyes (cartilaginous fish). Living Chondrichthyes include sharks, skates, rays and chimaeras.

Scales in Time
Prehistoric sharks had rows of tooth-like scales and non-permanent teeth like today's sharks.

You Don't Look a Day Over a Million
Many modern sharks are almost identical to ancient (extinct) species from 150 million years ago.

Pass the Plesiosaur
The discovery of teeth found embedded in 85- million-year-old fossilised bones of a plesiosaur is evidence of an ancient shark attack.

Bradyodonti

Cladoselachii

Gnathostoma

Euselachii

Elasmobrachii

Ctenacanthids

Osteichthyes (bony fish)

Actinopterygii

Chimaeriformes

Ground Sharks

Mackerel Sharks

Carpetsharks

Bullhead Sharks

Sawsharks

Angelsharks

Dogfish Sharks

Cow and Frilled Sharks

Rays and Skates

| 400 | 300 | 200 | 100 | 0 |

MILLIONS OF YEARS AGO

Wow, You're Old!
The oldest known intact shark skeleton (a *Doliodus problematicus*) was recently found in Canada. This shark lived 409 million years ago.

BEFORE WHALES, BEFORE BIRDS,
BEFORE DINOSAURS — 200 MILLION YEARS BEFORE DINOSAURS —
there were sharks. Sharks have rocked the seas for more than 400 million years. Tracing sharks throughout history is challenging because their cartilaginous skeleton is rarely preserved in fossils. Fortunately, fossilised teeth, scales and spines give paleontologists a sketchy view of prehistoric sharks. The oldest known sharks have been identified from scales found in rocks almost 455 million years ago.

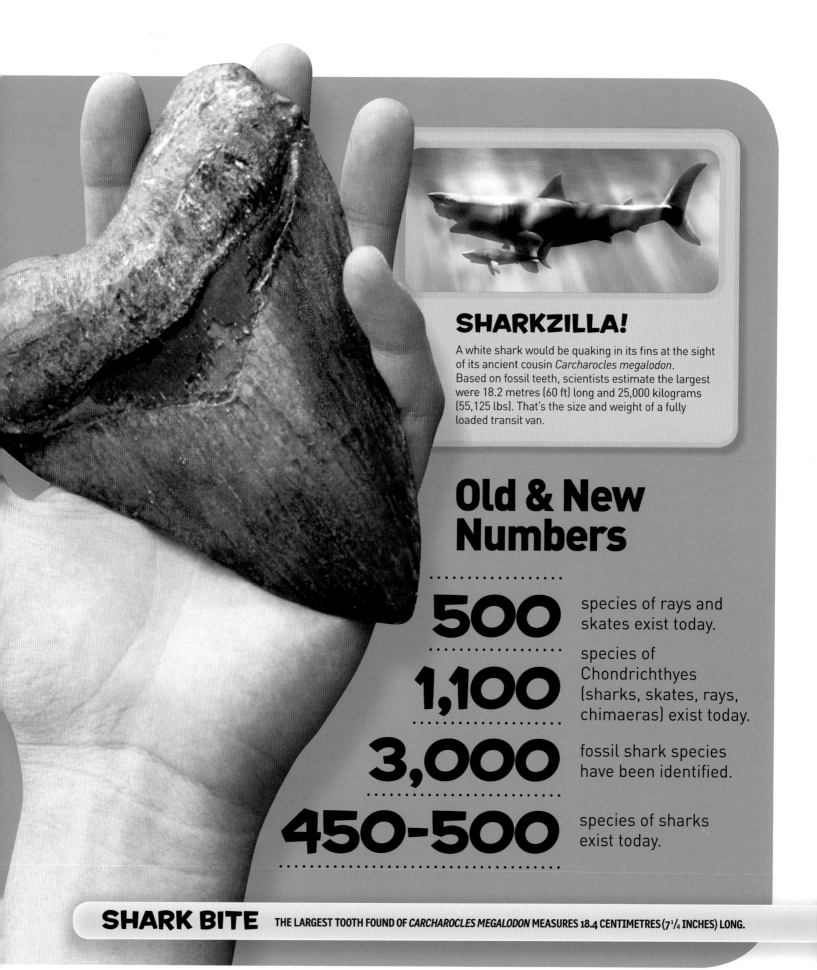

SHARKZILLA!

A white shark would be quaking in its fins at the sight of its ancient cousin *Carcharocles megalodon*. Based on fossil teeth, scientists estimate the largest were 18.2 metres (60 ft) long and 25,000 kilograms (55,125 lbs). That's the size and weight of a fully loaded transit van.

Old & New Numbers

500 species of rays and skates exist today.

1,100 species of Chondrichthyes (sharks, skates, rays, chimaeras) exist today.

3,000 fossil shark species have been identified.

450-500 species of sharks exist today.

SHARK BITE THE LARGEST TOOTH FOUND OF *CARCHAROCLES MEGALODON* MEASURES 18.4 CENTIMETRES (7¼ INCHES) LONG.

WEIRDEST SHARKS

SLEEK, ALOOF
SOPHISTICATED, ENERGETIC...

all part of a shark's DNA, right? As with all families, there are a few unattractive, quirky oddballs splashing around in the gene pool, too!

Sawsharks

Before it's even born, a sawshark's teeth erupt. Luckily for the mother, the teeth lay flat against the rostrum (snout) until after it's born.

Goblin Sharks

In the deep dark sea, the flabby, pinkish goblin shark floats and waits. When dinner swims near, the shark snaps with a speed and reach enhanced by flexible jaws that shoot forward, distorting its ghoulish appearance even more.

Greenland Sharks

The flesh of Greenland sharks is poisonous. This giant shark may snatch caribou right from the water's edge!

SHARK BITE STUDIES SHOW THAT A LEMON SHARK LEARNS 80 TIMES FASTER THAN A CAT!

Cookiecutter Sharks

Cookiecutter sharks add a twist to the camouflaging glow — an unlighted collar that lures prey. From below, the collar looks like a fish. When a would-be predator zooms in, the cookiecutter spins around and attacks first.

Lanternsharks

Ten percent of shark species are bioluminescent — they glow like a firefly. Light cells on the underside camouflage or hide the shark in the sunlight filtering down from above.

Frilled Sharks

Frilled sharks have changed very little since prehistoric times. These squid-eating, deep-sea sharks can grow as long as a Jeep. In 2009 scientists discovered a third frilled shark species.

OTHER ODDBALLS

Oceanic whitetip sharks hang out and hunt with pilot whales.

Shortfin makos are bright blue or purplish.

False eye spots on the backs of carpet sharks may trick predators.

Bull sharks occasionally swim 3,573 kilometres (2,220 miles) up the Amazon River (up to Peru) and 2,897 km (1,800 miles) up the Mississippi River all the way to Illinois.

Basking sharks, often found in British waters, grow to 6–8 metres (20–26 feet) in length.

Angel Sharks

Hiding beneath the sand, the angel shark sits perfectly still and patiently waits and waits and waits for prey. Some wait weeks until the right meal swims along.

BUSTING SHARK ATTACK MYTHS

An example of a provoked bite due to a diver feeding a shark near San Clemente Island, California, U.S.A.

PROVOKED vs. UNPROVOKED

Many shark 'attacks' are provoked or caused by people touching, grabbing, feeding or intentionally getting too close. Any wild animal can and will bite if frightened or threatened. A good rule of thumb: a shark is not a toy!

Because we share the shore with sharks, it sometimes leads to unprovoked attacks. Large sharks, such as white, tiger and bull, hunt large prey in warm coastal waters. And people swim and play in shallow, warm coastal waters. Sharks do not hunt people, but sometimes our playtime overlaps with their mealtime.

ATTACK... SUCH A BIG WORD

FOR A LITTLE BOO BOO. Turns out, worldwide in the last 50 years about 85% of 'attacks' are scratches and scrapes. To determine a more accurate level of injury, scientists and doctors have created a grading system (similar to what is used for burn victims): I (a scrape) to V (life threatening).

Scientists have identified three kinds of unprovoked attacks: hit-and-run, bump-and-bite and sneak. Hit-and-run often happens where people swim and surf. Most likely, the shark has mistaken the person for prey in the churned up water. As soon as it bites, it realises its error, takes off and does not return. Injuries are usually small and below the knee.

Bump-and-bite and sneak attacks usually happen in deeper water. In a bump-and-bite attack, the shark circles and bumps the victim before biting. In a sneak attack, the shark attacks without warning. In both cases, the shark bites more than once and the injuries are severe, often leading to death.

Still worried? In British coastal waters there have been very few shark attacks with only one known fatality at Hornsea, England in 1922.

MANY SHARKS STUFF THEMSELVES LIKE IT'S CHRISTMAS, THEN GO DAYS, EVEN WEEKS, BEFORE EATING AGAIN.

To a hungry shark looking up, a person on a body board might look like a tasty seal.

ATTACK FACTS

Sharks are portrayed as killing machines. But we seem to be the deadliest creature in the sea!

0–5
... people might be killed by sharks a year.

AN ESTIMATED 100,000,000
... sharks are killed by people every year.

YOUR NUMBER MIGHT BE UP

...but probably not because of a shark. Yes, sharks sometimes kill people. It's very rare. How rare? Chances of a shark fatally attacking a person are 1 in 3,748,067. Still worried about being attacked? Relax, you are more likely to:

- win *Britain's Got Talent*
- be struck by lightning
- die from the flu
- be killed by a deer
- hit a hole-in-one at golf
- drown (with no help from a shark)
- die in a bicycle accident
- be attacked by a crocodile
- be injured fixing a toilet
- get bitten by a spider
- be killed by fireworks
- die from a cold
- stub your toe
- die from a fall
- become a professional football player

...and the list goes on and on! (NOTE: The list is not in statistical order.)

SHARK BITE   BY BODY WEIGHT, A BONY FISH EATS TWICE AS MUCH AS A SHARK.

STUDYING SHARKS

At the Great Barrier Reef, Australia, researchers attach a satellite tag to the dorsal fin of a tiger shark.

A female oceanic whitetip shark takes a very close look at a scientist.

IT'S CHALLENGING TRYING
TO STUDY ANIMALS THAT ROUTINELY TRAVEL

hundreds, even thousands of miles or hide in the dark depths. Biologists use technology to virtually 'hangout' with sharks to reveal their secret world.

PLAYING TAG

Scientists followed Monty the mako shark 5,600-plus kilometres (3,500 miles) and a salmon shark named Goldilox more than 8,690 kilometres (5,400 miles) using electronic tags. Some tags track sharks in real time. The shark-GPS gives scientists up-to-the-minute data on a shark's location, distance, direction and swimming speed. Other kinds of tags store data, such as location, depth and water temperature, on a microchip. Scientists review the stored data after the chip falls off the shark.

CRITTERCAM

One might think it'd be a wild ride hanging out with tiger sharks, based on their reputation and diet. But Crittercam (a small camera temporarily attached to the shark) told a different story. Footage collected from tiger sharks showed them to be a bit boring, wandering through the sea in search of a trouble-free meal. No drama. No conflict. If the prey noticed the shark's approach, the tiger swam on, avoiding the extra work of fighting for its meal.

DNA

Analysing DNA from whale sharks from the Indian Ocean, Pacific Ocean and Caribbean Sea was like going to a family reunion. Turns out, though far apart, these populations were all closely related. That means whale sharks are interbreeding with others from distant parts of the world.

EXPLORERS' CORNER

A shark knows we're there before we have a clue about it. Once we were photographing dolphins in South Africa. A white shark that had probably watched us from the edge of visibility seemed to materialise out of nothing. Since we weren't in a cage we moved back to back to keep a 365-degree view of our guest. The curious shark made a wide circle and then vanished.

SHARK BITE   A SPINY DOGFISH CAN LIVE MORE THAN 100 YEARS.

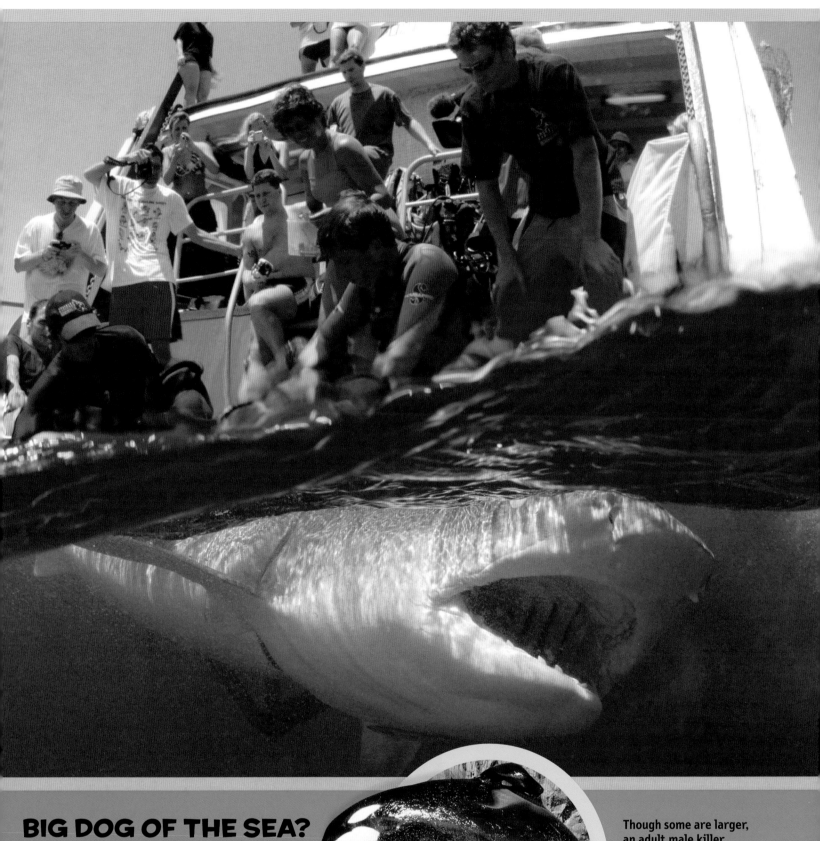

BIG DOG OF THE SEA?

People quake at the sight of a white shark . . . but white sharks might feel the same about killer whales (orca). After scientists observed a killer whale attack a white shark, all the white sharks in the area disappeared for several weeks.

Though some are larger, an adult male killer whale is about the same size as a large white shark — 5.8 to 6.7 metres (19-22 ft).

THE MOMENT A SHARK IS BORN,

IT CAN SWIM AND HUNT.

Its instant skill to dart, sprint and dive keeps it alive for the first hour, the first day. . . . Our lives are very different. Here are some examples.

SHARK COMPARISONS

YOU VS. A SHARK

FEARSOME FIN!

A large white shark's first dorsal fin is taller than 1 metre (3.2 ft) tall. That's taller than a 4-year-old child!

If you ate like a shark, you'd only eat a small meal, like a piece of pizza, every few days. (And, you'd have to swallow it whole!)

PREGNANCY

A human mum is pregnant for about 40 weeks.
A grey reef shark is pregnant for 52 weeks.

NOSE

Before it is even born, a lemon shark can smell
10,000 times better than you can right now.

SKIN

Because of the scales, a shark's skin feels like
sandpaper. Does yours?

PERMANENT TEETH

A shark starts losing teeth before it's even born, but it never has permanent teeth.
A six-year-old child starts replacing baby teeth with permanent teeth.

Don't let that silly grin fool you into getting too close. When pestered, a lemon shark will bite.

FUN
WITH
SHARKS

SWIM LIKE A SHARK

SOME SHARKS

RACE AT PHENOMENAL SPEEDS in pursuit of prey. Between hunts, they relax and cruise at much slower speeds of about 2.4 kilometres per hour (1.5 mph).

Ever wonder if you could outspeed a shark? Find out by measuring how far you swim (or run/walk) in five seconds. Compare your distance against the cruising and racing speeds of our sharks in a **Five Second Race**.

...a leopard shark would swim
2.7 METRES
(9 ft). That's about three rounders bats end-to-end.

...a 4.2-metre-long (14 ft) megamouth shark leisurely strolls
1.3 METRES
(4.25 ft). That's like moving over two seats in a football stadium.

0 METRES	8 METRES	15 METRES	23 METRES	31 M
(0 FT)	(25 FT)	(50 FT)	(75 FT)	(1

... a shortfin mako zips
73 METRES
(239 ft). On a football field, this speed demon could zoom from goal to goal. But the ball probably wouldn't survive!

GOLD MEDAL WINNER!

... a white shark can dash
56 METRES
(183 ft). That's more than a length of an Olympic-size swimming pool.

... a blue shark easily swims
53 METRES
(175 ft). It could sprint more than half a football pitch before the ref could blew the whistle and say, 'Shark on the field!'

... a quick 11-year-old can swim
6.1 METRES
(20 ft). On a basketball court, that's the distance from the free throw line to the court line.

HOW TO AVOID BEING SHARK BAIT

Avoid wearing your herring hat, blood sausage necklace and tuna-scented sunscreen... just kidding. To reduce the chances of accidentally meeting a shark experts suggest:

- Stay in groups and avoid swimming too far from shore.
- Avoid sunset or nighttime swims.
- Stay out of the water if sharks have been sighted.

- Avoid wearing bright colours (sharks see contrast very well) or shiny jewellery.
- Do not swim where sharks hunt (seal and sea lion rookeries, schools of fish, etc.).

- Do not touch, harass, grab or feed sharks.
- Avoid entering the water if you are bleeding.
- Avoid places where others are fishing or dragging their catch with them.

SHARK BITE MOST SHARKS ARE COLD-BLOODED, BUT SOME ARE WARM-BLOODED.

38 METRES (125 FT)	**46 METRES** (150 FT)	**53 METRES** (175 FT)	**61 METRES** (200 FT)	**69 METRES** (225 FT)	**76 METRES** (250 FT)

SPOT THE SHARKS

CHECK OUT
THESE STEALTHY SHARKS hiding in the rocks, sand and coral. Their camouflaging colours match the ocean floor. Blotches, spots and stripes also mimic the sunlight filtering through the water.

ABOVE: An ornate wobbegong from the South Pacific.

NEAR RIGHT: Curled up in defensive position, this puffadder shyshark, sometimes called a Happy Eddie, isn't so happy.

FAR RIGHT: Hiding under the sand, the Pacific angel shark is ready to ambush its prey.

TOP: A swell shark blends into the rocky California coast.

BOTTOM: Carpet sharks, like this Indonesian speckled carpet shark, can change colour to blend in even better.

SPOT THE WHALE SHARK

Scientists use a whale shark's spots to identify individuals. It's a bit like finding constellations in the night sky.

SHARK BITE   COMPARING TOOTH SIZE TO BODY SIZE, COOKIECUTTER SHARKS HAVE THE LARGEST TEETH OF ANY SHARK.

SHARKS IN CULTURE

BEFORE THEY WERE
FEARED, SHARKS WERE REVERED.
Today, with 24-hour news, the Internet, instant messaging and more, one shark bite becomes a global feeding frenzy of shark misinformation.

The irrational fear and hatred of sharks is new in human history. *Jaws* and other books, films, and television shows vaulted sharks into the limelight, forever changing their image from rare and fascinating ocean predators to man-eating monsters pacing just offshore awaiting tourist season.

Throughout history, sharks held a place of honour, often given the role as protector or guardian. Sharks are represented in the art and tradition of the indigenous people of Hawaii, the Bidjogo people from Africa, the Aboriginal people of Australia, the Maori of New Zealand and the Kuna people of the Panamanian islands. Swordfish, sharks and rays were even found buried beneath an Aztec temple in Mexico City.

A shark carving from the Makira Province in the Solomon Islands

SHARK BITE   THEY MAY HAVE AN ENORMOUS REPUTATION, BUT MOST SHARKS ARE ONLY THE SIZE OF A BASEBALL BAT!

SPUD SHARK STAMPS

Show your shark spirit by making a shark stamp. Here's how:

Child-safe tempura paint

Pumpkin-carving tools or plastic utensils

Potato   **Paper**   **Paintbrush**

1 Ask an adult to cut the potato in half.

2 Etch a shark shape into the potato, then carve out the shape. You can carve around the shark shape or dig out the shape. Either way works.

3 Spread paint across carving.

4 Press onto paper. Lift. Enjoy!

5 Make prints, a journal, notepaper. . . . do not eat the potato.

Popular films such as *Finding Nemo* and *Jaws* portray sharks in different ways. LEFT: The shark is a mechanical model.

PLACES TO SAFELY SEE SHARKS

**Deep Sea World, Scotland,
Blue Planet Aquarium, England
SeaLife Centres
Oregon Coast Aquarium, U.S.A.
Ocean World, Australia**

Visit the SeaLife Aquariums
website [https://www.visitsealife.
com/] to find an aquarium
near you.

FIN-TASTIC VIEW!

IF STANDING ON THE OCEAN FLOOR

WATCHING A SHARK GLIDE OVERHEAD SOUNDS APPEALING, THEN AN AQUARIUM IS FOR YOU.

Aquariums raise appreciation and concern for animals. Plus, biologists learn about behaviour, diet, food intake and reproduction; knowledge that helps us better understand all sharks. Aquariums throughout the world are adding new dimensions so people can get closer to the sharks. Some have giant viewing areas, like the four-story-tall Giant Ocean Tank at the New England Aquarium, U.S.A. Others have acrylic tunnels where the sharks swim over and alongside you.

You can even put on a wetsuit and swim with sand tiger sharks, lemon sharks, nursing sharks, bamboo sharks and wobbegongs at the Blue Planet Aquarium in Cheshire, U.K. There, the sharks are carefully monitored, well fed (i.e. not hungry for you), and used to people in the water.

Tourists enjoy the breathtaking view of sharks in an aquarium viewing tunnel.

FIN FUN

Whether it's an on-the-go hunter, a low-key drifter or a bottom-dwelling shark, the fins tell you about a shark's lifestyle. Can you determine its swimming style by matching the tail to the shark?

Mako
FASTEST

Horn Shark
BOTTOM DWELLER

Catshark
SLOW

Blue Shark
FAST

Frilled Shark
SLUGGISH

Whitetip Reef Shark
WEAK SWIMMER

 1

 2

 3

 4

 5

 6

SHARK BITE THE SHARK TUNNEL AT DEEP SEA WORLD IN SCOTLAND IS 112 METRES (367 FT) LONG. THAT'S ABOUT THE LENGTH OF A FOOTBALL PITCH!

ANSWERS: Mako: 2; Horn Shark: 4; Catshark: 5; Blue Shark: 3; Frilled Shark: 6; Whitetip Reef Shark: 1

PHOTO FINISH

WORKING IN SHARK-

INFESTED WATERS ISN'T JUST AN
expression, it's a normal day at work for
photographers like David Doubilet and Jennifer
Hayes.

Photographing sharks requires extensive
planning and packing, travelling to remote
areas and spending weeks at sea and hours
underwater. Photographers must know the
environment, the kinds of sharks in the area,
whether they should snorkel or dive and
whether they need a boat or even a shark cage.

It's physical work to get close to the sharks, too.
Photographers must swim, snorkel, scramble
across rocky shores or wade in shallow water
while carrying cameras and other equipment.

After all that work and prep, sometimes the
sharks never appear. But when everything works
right, and the photographer is able to capture
the majesty of a shark in a single photograph,
it motivates, inspires and encourages people
to look at sharks in a new way.

**Looking for sharks in new places
and spaces, scientists come
across a sleeping reef shark in an
ocean cavern in the Gulf
of Mexico. David Doubilet
captured this magical moment.**

AFTERWORD

CONSERVATION CONCERNS

Nets set for other fish often trap sharks.

SHARKS ARE AS IMPORTANT TO THE SEA AS THE WATER ITSELF.

THERE'S NO DOUBT THAT FOR THE LAST 400 MILLION YEARS, sharks and their relatives have shaped ocean ecosystems. From meteors, volcanoes, ice ages and continents moving and separating, sharks have endured every catastrophic change. But they may not survive their most dangerous challenge — people.

Every hour, 11,415 sharks are killed for their fins, meat, skin, liver oil (squalene), cartilage, teeth, and sometimes accidentally. Products boasting the health and beauty benefits of shark oil and cartilage have flooded markets worldwide.

Annually an estimated 100 million sharks, including hammerhead, blue, mako, basking and dogfish, die for soup. The fins are cut off, then the shark is dumped into the sea to die.

In recent years there has been growing opposition to finning. The European Union and a number of countries have banned it.

Take an interest in shark preservation. Visit www.sharktrust.org for more information.

The sea feeds the world. Finding a balance between conservation and consumption is at the heart of sustainable fishing practices.

Worldwide, there is little or no regulation or protection. As shark hunting increases, populations decrease. The number of sharks has dropped by 90 percent in the Gulf of Mexico and 75 percent in the northwestern Atlantic. In the Mediterranean, more than 40 percent of sharks and rays are threatened with extinction.

Because sharks reproduce so slowly, even if shark fisheries stopped today, scientists worry populations may not rebound.

PLASTIC THREAT TO SHARKS

IN RECENT YEARS there has been growing concern about sharks and other marine life ingesting large quantities of plastic fragments known as microplastics. This is in the form of micro beads from personal care products, fibres from clothes and large plastic items which gradually break into small pieces. This exposes sharks to toxic chemicals. Plastic is now entering every level of the ocean food chain and can end up in the seafood we eat.

Worldwide, marine life campaign groups are promoting bans on microplastics in products that enter drains like wet wipes, detergents and sun screen to stop them reaching the oceans.

Why don't you get involved in stopping plastics polluting the sea and putting marine life in danger?

The silky shark's name describes its skin texture. Overlapping scales are so tightly packed together the skin feels smooth.

AN INTERACTIVE GLOSSARY

A sicklefin lemon shark scatters a school of blue-striped snappers.

WANT TO SOUND LIKE A

SHARK EXPERT? These words will help. Check out the glossary word, test your shark knowledge, then follow the page numbers to see the word in 'action'.

Adaptation
(PAGES 10-11, 16-17, 18-19, 24-25, 36-37)
A body part or behaviour that helps an animal survive.

Which adaptation leads to millions of shark deaths?
a. fins
b. teeth
c. scales
d. skin

Bioluminescence
(PAGE 37)
An adaptation that allows an animal to create or use light for camouflage, to find food, attract a mate or as an alarm.

What percentage of sharks are bioluminescent?
a. 50%
b. 1%
c. 10%
d. 25%

Camouflage
(PAGES 16-17, 18-19, 37, 48-49)
Colour, pattern and/or body shape that helps an animal hide or blend into its surroundings.

Which of these sharks hides on the seabed for weeks waiting for a meal?
a. porbeagle
b. salmon shark
c. whitetip reef shark
d. angel shark

Cartilage
(PAGES 10-11, 34-35, 56-57)
Flexible but sturdy tissue that shapes our ears, nose and a shark's skeleton.

Sharks' cartilaginous skeleton adds to the challenges of understanding them because . . .
a. cartilage is rarely found in fossils.
b. it limits the shark's size.
c. it's so flimsy, scientists can't touch sharks.
d. Both b and c.

Chondrichthyes
(PAGES 34-35)
The class of cartilaginous fishes that includes sharks, skates, rays and chimaeras.

What is the largest kind of Chondrichthyes?
a. white shark
b. manta ray
c. whale shark
d. basking shark

Embryo
(PAGES 22-23)
A baby animal developing inside an egg or female.

In some species, if a shark embryo absorbs the entire yolk sac it...
a. does not survive.
b. is born early.
c. eats the other eggs inside the mother.

Habitat
(PAGES 14-15, 16-17)
A plant's or animal's home.

Which habitat is a shark's home?
a. sandy beach
b. coral reef
c. freshwater river
d. all of the above

Pup
(PAGES 16-17, 22-23)
A newborn or young shark.

What do shark mothers feed their pups?
a. milk
b. nothing
c. chewed up fish
d. sardines

Predator and Prey
(PAGES 26-27)
A predator hunts and eats other animals. Prey is the animal that is eaten.

What is a favourite food of many sharks?
a. other sharks
b. seaweed
c. people
d. krill

Species
(PAGES 10-11, 12-13, 14-15, 16-17, 34-35, 36-37)
Scientists categorise or group plants and animals to help study and understand them. The categories start with a large general grouping, such as animals or plants (kingdom) down to the most specific or unique adaptations — species (kingdom, phylum, class, order, family, genus, species).

How many of the 32,000 species of fish are sharks?
a. 20,000
b. 40
c. 500
d. 1,000

Spiracle
(PAGES18-19)
Openings on top of a shark's or ray's head that brings water over the gills.

This adaptation is especially helpful to . . .
a. whale sharks because it's hard to filter food and breathe.
b. bottom-dwelling sharks and rays so they can breathe without getting a mouthful of sand.
c. none of the above

Squalene
(PAGES 18-19, 56)
A high-quality oil from a shark's liver.

Compared to its body weight, how big is a basking shark's liver?
a. 15%
b. 25%
c. 50%
d. 3%

Tagging
(PAGES 40-41)
Attaching radio or satellite tags to an animal to track its movement.

True or False: A satellite tag does *not* provide up-to-the-minute information on a shark's location.

a. True
b. False

ANSWERS: Adaptation: a; Bioluminescence: a; Camouflage: c; Cartilage: d; Chondrichthyes: c; Embryo: c; Habitat: d; Pup: b; Predator and Prey: a; Species: a; Squalene: c; Spiracle: b; Tagging: b

FIND OUT MORE

Love sharks and want to go deeper? Try these books and websites to learn everything else about sharks.

BOOK TITLES WITH A BITE

Sharks of the World
BY LEONARD COMPAGNO, MARC DANDO, AND SARAH FOWLER.
Princeton: Princeton University Press, 2005.

Face to Face with Sharks
BY DAVID DOUBILET AND JENNIFER HAYES.
Washington, DC: National Geographic, 2009.

WEBSITES

Shark Bites
https://www.bbc.co.uk/cbbc/shows/shark-bites

Natural History Museum, London
https://blog.nhm.ac.uk/tag/shark-tooth/

Australian Museum
https://australianmuseum.net.au/sharks

International Shark Attack Files
www.flmnh.ufl.edu/fish/sharks/isaf/isafabout.htm

Shark Trust
https://www.sharktrust.org

BOLDFACE INDICATES ILLUSTRATIONS.

To REM, I miss you every day. RM

Acknowledgments
Thank you to all the dedicated researchers working to save the sharks. A special thanks to Jeremy Vaudo, Florida International University; Dr Tom Deméré, San Diego Natural History Museum; and Dr Tamara Frank, Harbor Branch Oceanographic Institute/Florida Atlantic University. Your insight and knowledge were invaluable.

Prepared by the Book Division
Nancy Laties Feresten, *Vice President,*
   Editor in Chief, Children's Books
Jonathan Halling, *Design Director, Children's Publishing*
Jennifer Emmett, *Executive Editor, Children's Books*
Carl Mehler, *Director of Maps*
R. Gary Colbert, *Production Director*
Jennifer A. Thornton, *Managing Editor*

Staff for This Book
Jennifer Emmett, Priyanka Lamichhane, *Project Editors*
Eva Absher-Schantz, *Art Director*
Lori Epstein, Annette Kiesow, *Illustrations Editors*
Erin Mayes, Chad Tomlinson, *Designers*
Kate Olesin, *Editorial Assistant*
Grace Hill, *Associate Managing Editor*
Lewis R. Bassford, *Production Manager*
Susan Borke, *Legal and Business Affairs*
Madeleine Franklin, *Editorial Intern*
Janice Gilman, *Illustrations Intern*

Manufacturing and Quality Management
Christopher A. Liedel, *Chief Financial Officer*
Phillip L. Schlosser, *Senior Vice President*
Chris Brown, *Technical Director*
Nicole Elliott, *Manager*
Rachel Faulise, *Manager*
Robert L. Barr, *Manager*

Captions
Front Cover: A great white shark shows his razor-sharp teeth as he thrashes out of the water.
Back Cover: Hammerhead sharks, Cocos Islands.
Page 1: Caribbean reef sharks glide over a coral reef in the Bahamas.
Pages 2-3: Beautiful blue sharks silhouetted in the California sun.

Published by Collins
An imprint of HarperCollins Publishers
Westerhill Road
Bishopbriggs
Glasgow G64 2QT
www.harpercollins.co.uk

In association with National Geographic Partners, LLC

NATIONAL GEOGRAPHIC and the Yellow Border Design are trademarks of the National Geographic Society, used under license.

Second edition 2018
First published 2011

ISBN 978-0-00-826775-9

10 9 8 7 6 5 4 3

Printed in Great Britain by Bell & Bain Ltd, Glasgow

If you would like to comment on any aspect of this book, please contact us at the above address or online.
natgeokidsbooks.co.uk
collins.reference@harpercollins.co.uk

Paper from responsible sources

Since 1888, the National Geographic Society has funded more than 12,000 research, exploration, and preservation projects around the world. The Society receives funds from National Geographic Partners, LLC, funded in part by your purchase. A portion of the proceeds from this book supports this vital work. To learn more, visit natgeo.com/info.